P9-DHD-474

One Single Species

Why the Connections in Nature Matter

Susan E. Quinlan

Raven Mountain

Bellvue • Colorado

First Edition, 2020

Publisher's Cataloging-In-Publication Data
(Prepared by The Donohue Group, Inc.)

Names: Quinlan, Susan E., author.
Title: One single species : why the connections in nature matter / Susan E. Quinlan.
Description: First edition. | Bellvue, Colorado : Raven Mountain Press, 2020. | Interest age level: 10 and up. | Summary: "Describes the historic field experiments of a scientist whose research led to a better understanding of the ecological importance of individual species"--Provided by publisher.
Identifiers: ISBN 9780997007749 (hardback) | ISBN 9780997007763 (paperback) | ISBN 9780997007725 (ebook)
Subjects: LCSH: Paine, Robert T., 1933-2016--Knowledge--Keystone species--Juvenile literature. | Keystone species--Research--Juvenile literature. | Intertidal ecology--Research--Juvenile literature. | Marine biology--Research--Juvenile literature. | CYAC: Paine, Robert T., 1933-2016--Knowledge--Keystone species. | Keystone species--Research. | Ecology--Research. | Marine biology--Research.
Classification: LCC QH541.14 .Q56 2020 (print) | LCC QH541.14 (ebook) | DDC 577.26--dc23

Sincere thanks to Dr. Robert T. Paine who provided input on early versions of the manuscript and artwork prior to his death, and to Dr. Christopher Harley (and his daughter, Zoe), Dr. Tim Wootton, Dr. Bruce A. Menge, and Dr. Paul Dayton for their thoughtful and constructive input on draft versions of this book.

A heartfelt thank you to Anne Paine for permission to include her photo of Dr. Paine and to both Anne Wertheim Rosenfeld and William A. Lehnhausen for allowing me to use their wonderful photographs for art reference.
I am grateful to the many writer and educator friends who offered suggestions and comments which helped shape this book and encouraged me along the way. I also thank my editor, Gin Walker, for all her helpful contributions to this project.

A portion of all proceeds from this book donated to the Robert T. Paine Experimental and Field Ecology Endowed Fund at the University of Washington to assist students undertaking ecological research.

FSC
www.fsc.org
MIX
Paper from responsible sources
FSC® C004755

Printed in the United States of America
on Forest Stewardship Council
Certified Paper

To all the creatures
with whom we humans
share our Earth

and to

Robert T. Paine
who conducted the years of field research
upon which this book is based.

Wham! A twenty foot high ocean wave pounds the rocky Washington coast. The raging waters scour the shore with a force more powerful than a hurricane. Along this coast, the slippery crags are treacherous, the thundering waves, a peril.

When the tide is high, few signs of ocean life are present. Glaucous-winged gulls perch on the high rocks at the ocean's edge, or sail crying overhead. Scattered flocks of scoters and harlequin ducks bob on the angry ocean surface, diving now and then beneath the roiling sea. The massive waves dominate the scene.

This noisy and dangerous place seems an unlikely site for a scientist to learn about the connections among living things. Yet this is the place where ecologist Dr. Robert T. Paine (Bob to his friends) undertook a landmark study which changed the way biologists think about ecosystems and individual species.

The incessant waves keep the natural world that Bob studied inaccessible and hidden most of the time. But twice a day, the tide recedes and the scene changes.

The scoters fly out to sea with
the waves to bob together in
rafts beyond the breakers. The
harlequin ducks feed in the
shallows at first, then shake
the water from their wings and
clamber on to rocks to rest until
the waves return.

At the lowest tides, rocks that lay
drowning under several feet of
ocean just hours earlier, are now
left high and dry, exposed to the
sun and wind.

Bob observed a fascinating
ecosystem of algae and animals
in this intertidal zone revealed by
the rolled back sea.

Everywhere along Washington's rocky coast, the intertidal life exists in a predictable vertical pattern.

Crusty white barnacles carpet the rocks along the uppermost edge of every wave-scoured shore. In some areas, a band of yellow rockweed grows below the barnacles. Beneath the rockweed, a dense carpet of blue-brown California mussels forms a wide band.

Farther down yet, in the lower intertidal zone, an explosion of diverse creatures flourish. Volcano-shaped limpets, multi-colored snails and whelks, spiny sea urchins, chitons, sea cucumbers, sponges, sea anemones and sea stars intermingle with an array of seaweeds and brilliant pink coralline algae.

Season to season, year in and year out, at each low tide, this intertidal scene remains much the same. To an untrained observer, it looks like nothing much is going on. But Bob, an experienced ecologist, knew that here, like everywhere in nature, things are always happening. You just have to take time to look.

Bob knew he could measure the patches of algae and stalks of seaweed on the rocks and find changes over time. These plant-like organisms continually grow – converting air, water and energy from sunlight into food for themselves and other creatures through photosynthesis.

At low tide, Bob watched surfbirds and turnstones poking around the seaweeds to pick out small creatures left stranded by the waves.

Black oystercatchers probed amidst the rocks with orange chisel-like bills. A limpet or chiton here, a mussel there, met its end in an oyster-catcher's stomach.

Gulls often wheeled in the winds that frosted the distant waves in white. The gulls landed to dine on barnacles, limpets, and sea urchins. Once in a while, Bob spotted a gull tugging a mussel from the rocks, kiting upward on the wind, then dropping it. The mussel's hard shell shattered on impact, allowing the gull to feast.

The lively motions of the birds were not what most interested the scientist however. He was more curious about the intertidal animals that disappeared twice each day, beneath the rolling waves.

When exposed to the air and sun, most of these don't even look alive. They don't move much, if at all, because they are water creatures and must stay wet to live.

When the falling tide leaves them exposed to air, they must hunker down, clenching whatever water they can hold. Motionless, they await the return of their ocean home.

To observe these underwater creatures going about their lives, Bob peered into tidepools – ponds of water left behind by the receding sea.

Gooseneck Barnacles

Acorn Barnacles

In the pools, Bob saw barnacles open their shells and wave fan-like limbs through the water to sweep in their prey – tiny, waterborne algae and animals, called plankton.

He observed mussels feeding too. These animals open their shells to extend fleshy mantles. These help guide swirling seawater into the mussel, past inner nets of sticky mucus that trap floating plankton.

California Mussels

Pink Sponges

Coralline Algae

Purple Sea Urchin

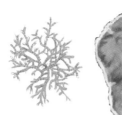
Limpet

Chiton

Bob examined the sponges and coralline algae that covered rock surfaces in hues of pink. He noted purple sea urchins using special tooth-like mouthparts to graze on algae and drifting seaweed.

With great patience, Bob watched limpets and chitons slink over tidepool rocks, using rasping tongues to scrape off algae.

He watched anemones unfold and wave flower-like tentacles tipped with stinging cells. These waving tentacles stun and capture small animals swept past by the seawater.

Larger and less common animals also hunted in the tidepools. Predatory snails, called whelks, glided over the rocks. Sometimes Bob noticed one attacking its prey. More often he noticed the telltale holes drilled through the empty shells of animals these snails had eaten.

Sea Anemone

Whelks

Mussel Shell with telltale hole left by a predatory snail

One of the largest predators, the ochre sea star (also known by its scientific name, *Pisaster ochraceus*), fascinated Bob. These orange, yellow-brown, or purple animals use their suction cup-lined arms to maneuver over the intertidal rocks in search of prey. When a sea star finds a stationary or slower-moving animal, it uses its powerful arms to pull the animal off the rock. Sometimes the sea star carries its prey to another spot. Sometimes it dines immediately. Wherever it chooses to feed, the sea star hunkers down atop its prey. Extending its stomach outside its own body, it then engulfs and digests the trapped creature.

Bob noticed that limpets and snails could glide away from the approaching maw of these creeping predators. And often they escaped.

14

In contrast, California mussels, the sea star's favorite prey, rarely survived an attack. Anchored to the rocks by byssal threads which hold them in place amidst the surging waves, a mussel cannot move away – not even slowly. Mussels can only escape a hungry sea star if they are too large to be engulfed.

Bob began to wonder what would happen on the rocky shore, and in the tidepools, if ochre sea stars weren't there. Would the populations of mussels increase without sea stars around to eat them? Would other predators, like whelks, switch their prey and eat more mussels?

What difference would it make if this one single species disappeared from this ecosystem? As a scientist, Bob didn't just wonder. He set up an experiment to find the answer.

For his study areas, Bob selected stretches of isolated, rocky coast where visitors would not disturb his research. He divided the areas into two sections: control areas and experimental areas.

He counted and recorded the numbers and kinds of algae and animals living in sample plots in all the areas to ensure the sites were comparable.

Next, Bob made one simple change in his experimental areas. When the tide was out, the scientist clambered around the slippery rocks and pried off all the ochre sea stars he could find. He put them back in the ocean away from his experimental areas.

In the control areas, he left the sea stars alone.

For several years, Bob revisited the study plots when the tide was at its lowest levels. He visited every two weeks during the summers, and once a month during winter. On each visit, he removed any ochre sea stars that had moved into his experimental areas. Over the years, he removed thousands of sea stars and watched carefully for any changes in the interidal life of his study areas.

At first Bob didn't notice any changes.

On the intertidal rocks of Bob's control areas, the marine life remained unchanged over the years. The same interesting variety of algae and marine animals that had flourished at the beginning of his study continued to thrive.

But just months into his study, the scientist noticed a change in the experimental areas where he had removed the sea stars.

Early in their life cycle, larval mussels swim around as plankton. When they turn into adult form, they grab tight to barnacles or other mussels with their byssal threads.

Mussel larvae had not survived in the lower intertidal zone before. But without predation by sea stars, young mussels began to flourish and grow there.

Soon the mussels formed such a thick carpet in the lower intertidal zone that they crowded out almost all the other creatures!

This surprised Bob. He had not expected that the removal of one single predator species would cause such a remarkable change.

More than 26 species of anemones, chitons, urchins, limpets, whelks, and algae that had thrived in the lower intertidal zone no longer had space to live. They were completely crowded out by the mussels.

Bob expected that other mussel predators, like whelks, would soon move in to his experimental areas and thin the mussel carpet. He thought that would allow the ecosystem to eventually return to its former state. So he continued to remove sea stars from his experimental plots for another five years.

His prediction was wrong. Over that entire five years, the California mussels continued to thrive in all the experimental areas he kept free of sea stars. And none of the many displaced species returned. Some new kinds of small creatures that could live among the mussels did move in. But without sea stars, the lower intertidal ecosystem remained dramatically different.

This experiment showed that removing just one species can affect an entire ecosystem and cause unexpected changes in the populations of many other species.

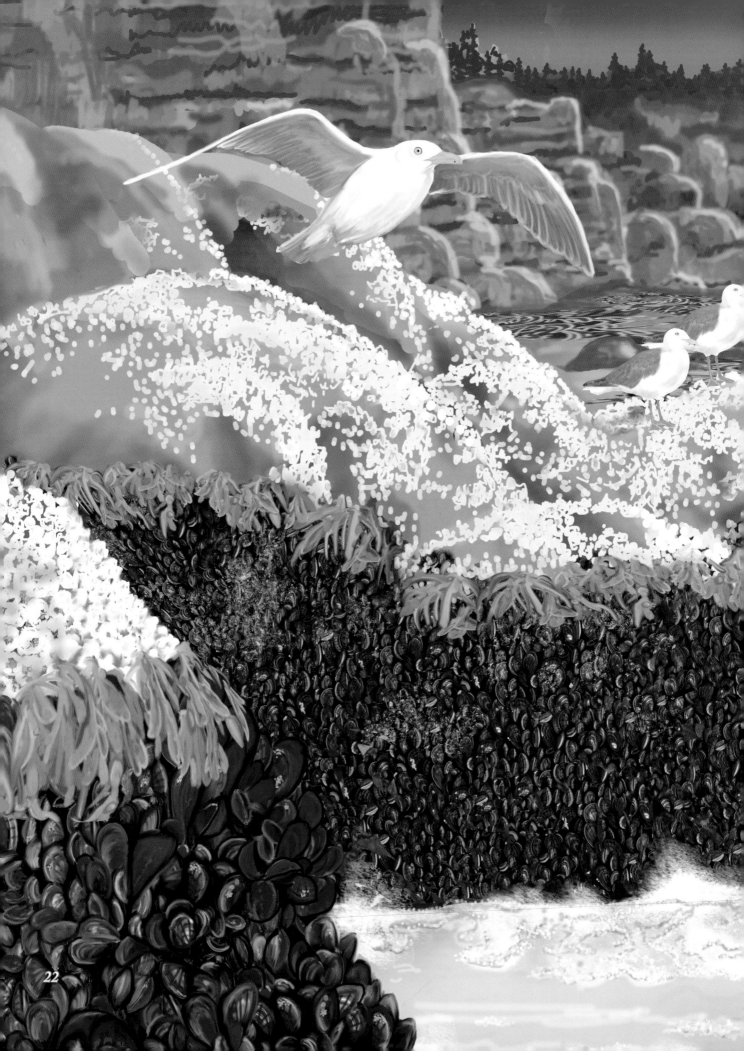

This was a startling discovery. Up until then, scientists had not supposed that any single species could be that important in shaping an ecosystem.

So Bob wanted to be doubly sure about what had occurred. What would happen if sea stars returned to the experimental areas? Would that allow the return of all the intertidal creatures that had once lived there? To find out, Bob stopped removing ochre sea stars from his experimental areas.

At first, nothing happened. Many of the mussels thriving in the lower intertidal zone had grown far too large for sea stars to eat. Not even a large sea star, or a throng of them, could put a dent in the thickets of big mussels.

As a result, the dense mussel carpets remained intact for many years after Bob stopped removing the sea stars. Some of the largest mussels still survived in his experimental areas even thirty years later!

Eventually, however, the relentless pounding of the waves and the deaths of old mussels created open spaces in the mussel beds. Then things began to change. The sea stars kept these openings clear by preying on any new mussels that tried to settle. Gradually, algae, chitons, snails, anemones, and other species moved into the open spaces.

Bob coined the term "keystone species" to describe the critically important role of ochre sea stars in Washington's rocky intertidal ecosystem. A keystone is the top block in a stone archway. Without it, the whole archway collapses.

With a new perspective on the potential importance of individual species, scientists began to look for keystone species in many other ecosystems around the world.

25

You can't easily see what is going on when you visit any of Earth's many ecosystems – an ocean, a forest, a prairie, a desert, or a wetland. You must take time to make careful observations.

You will have to watch for a long time to notice the plants growing. You might see plant-eating animals feeding, but you will be lucky to spot a predator killing its prey. While many of the organisms may be competing with each other over space to live or food to eat, you aren't likely to perceive their struggles.

You won't notice insects transporting pollen, or see birds or other animals helping scatter seeds unless you're watching very carefully. And without a microscope, no one can see the billions of bacteria, fungi, and protozoans that exist in every ecosystem.

Your observations might lead you to suppose that nothing much would change if just one single species disappeared. Many people, even biologists, once thought this. Dr. Robert T. Paine's research changed that.

Bob's study proved that what is going on in an ecosystem matters. The complex interactions among all living things are what shape and maintain the world around us.

The important role of any single species may be impossible to understand unless that species is removed or disappears.

Then, quite suddenly, the archways of nature which that species shaped or held together can dramatically shift. And many unrelated species, even entire ecosystems, can be affected, or even lost.

All due to the disappearance of one single species.

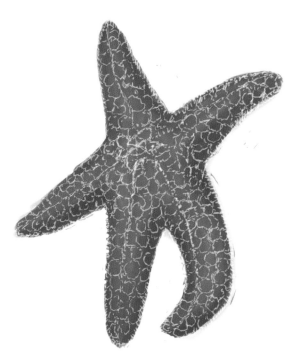

Dr. Robert T. Paine
April 13, 1933 - June 13, 2016

Bob Paine grew up near Cambridge, Massachusetts. He loved being outdoors in nature from the time he was a young boy. Bob remembered being fascinated by the ants in his parents' driveway when he was only 2½ years old. He enjoyed seeing and identifying wild birds even as a youngster. His ability to pay attention to details in nature served him well when he became an adult.

Bob attended Harvard University to earn his undergraduate college degree. He hoped to pursue a career in paleontology, the study of fossils. But while working toward an advanced degree in this topic at the University of Michigan, Bob became intrigued by ecology and soon switched his major.

Photo by: Anne Paine

After obtaining his PhD, Bob began his career as a Professor of Zoology at the University of Washington in 1962. Shortly thereafter he started working on his now historic studies of *Pisaster ochraceus*, the ochre sea star, and other intertidal life of the Pacific coast.

Bob's scientific discoveries and insights on the role of sea stars in intertidal ecosystems changed the way scientists around the world look at nature. His methods also changed the way many scientists study ecosystems. Where biologists once tried to learn mainly through observation, Bob's example showed how to learn more by setting up careful experiments in nature to test ideas.

Bob received worldwide recognition and many prestigious science awards for his research, including the MacArthur Award for lifetime achievement from the Ecological Society of America, the ECI prize from the Ecology Institute in Germany, and the International Cosmos Prize. He wrote and co-authored many articles and several books about nature during his lifetime.

Aside from his personal contributions to the science of ecology, his most enduring legacy may be his dedicated work as a biology professor. Over forty years, Bob mentored and inspired many young students who then followed in his footsteps, developing strong skills as field biologists and conducting their own experiments to help us all better understand how nature works.

In honor of Bob, and to help support and encourage even more students to get out in the field and learn about nature firsthand, a portion of all proceeds from this book will be donated to the Robert T. Paine Experimental and Field Ecology Endowed Fund. This fund supports research travel and purchase of supplies by University of Washington Department of Biology graduate students engaged in field research.

The more we learn about nature, the more likely that we humans can figure out ways to keep our planet healthy and beautiful, full of remarkable creatures and thriving ecosystems.

Glossary

algae — a group of organisms made up of one to many cells which are capable of photosynthesis. In contrast to plants, algae do not have specialized stems, leaves, roots and reproductive structures.

biologist — a scientist who studies living things.

byssal thread — strong, silk-like fibers produced by mussels to anchor themselves to rocks and other surfaces to avoid getting washed away by the sea.

coastal — occurring along the land edge, or coast, of an island or continent.

connection — a tie, or interaction, between or among living organisms, or between organisms and the nonliving environment; a synonym for interaction

control area — a place where nothing is changed, in contrast to an experimental area where one or more things are changed to find out what happens as a result.

interaction — an action or influence between or among living organisms, or between organisms and the nonliving environment; a synonym for connection

ecologist — a scientist who studies ecology.

ecology — the science of studying ecosystems, focusing on the interactions among living things and the nonliving environment.

ecosystem — all of the living and nonliving things in a particular environment and their interactions. This includes all plants, animals, fungi, microscopic organisms, and the air, water, soil, sunlight, and the ways in which all of these interact and affect each other.

experiment — a way to determine the answer to a specific question by comparing the differences or changes that result from modifying one or more variables.

experimental area — an area in which one or more variables are changed so that a scientist can determine the effects of the change or changes.

intertidal zone — coastal land that is repeatedly exposed and submerged due to daily changes in water depth caused by the rise and fall of the tide.

invertebrate — any kind of animal that lacks a backbone.

keystone — generally refers to the top block in a stone archway. In ecology, it now refers to any living thing whose presence or absence has a powerful effect on the ecosystem where it naturally occurs.

ochre — a yellow-brown to orange color. Ochre is used to name the sea star this book is about because the animal's scientific name is *Pisaster ochraceus*. Individuals may be yellow-brown, orange, or purple. Sometimes the name "purple sea star" is used for this same species.

photosynthesis — the chemical process used by plants and algae to combine water, carbon dioxide, and energy from sunlight to form sugars and release oxygen.

plankton — small and microscopic animals and algae which float or drift in water

rockweed — a common name for a specific kind of brown algae.

seaweed — a general term referring to any type of multi-celled algae that grows in a sea or ocean.

species — a group of living things with particular traits which can produce young with the same traits.

tidal — relating to the tide.

tide — the alternating rise and fall of the surface of the ocean or other large body of water caused mainly by the gravitational pull of the moon and sun.

tidepool — a small or large pond of seawater which remains when the tide goes out and leaves surrounding rocks exposed to the air.

variable — a factor that is changed in an experiment to determine what changes occur as a result.

About the birds in this book

Bob Paine enjoyed seeing and learning about birds from a young age. While his studies focused mainly on sea stars and other invertebrates, he always had a keen interest in birds. Among the most obvious and active animals along the coast, birds are easy and fun to learn to identify. They inspire and intrigue us with their ability to fly, their long migrations, and their adaptations for life in many different environments.

Black Oystercatcher

Male and female oystercatchers look alike. With a bright orange bill, red-rimmed yellow eyes, and pink legs, these otherwise black birds are easy to identify. They make loud raucous cries, often traveling in groups along rocky shores of the outer coast. They live year-round along the rocky North Pacific coast from Mexico to Alaska.

Haematopus bachmani

Length: 16–18 1/2 inches
Weight: 25 ounces

Calidris virgata

Length: 9–9 1/2 inches
Weight: 5–6 1/2 ounces

Surfbird

Surfbirds are named for their habit of roosting and feeding on the outer rocks of the coast close to the pounding surf. These long-distance migrants occur along the Washington coast while moving between their nesting grounds in the alpine tundra of Alaska and wintering areas along the coast as far south as the Strait of Magellan at the tip of South America.

Black Turnstone

Turnstones feed on small invertebrates which they pry off intertidal rocks. Their dark coloration can make them difficult to spot while feeding and roosting on wave-splashed rocks. But their black and white wing and tail markings flash brightly when they fly. Black turnstones nest in wetlands and tundra of coastal Alaska. They occur along the rocky Pacific coast from southeast Alaska to central Mexico.

Arenaria melanocephala

Length: 9–9 1/4 inches
Weight: 4 1/2 ounces

Harlequin Duck

A harlequin is a clown-like character who wears a multi-colored costume. This duck is named for its striking coloration. Patches of rusty brown contrast with its blue-gray feathers. The bird shown is a male. Females are more drab. Harlequin ducks live along rocky shores in the northern North Pacific and North Atlantic during most of the year, but migrate inland to nest along mountain streams in summer. They feed on aquatic invertebrates which they catch by diving underwater.

Histrionicus histrionicus

Length: 13–21 inches
Weight: 17–25 ounces

Black Scoter

One of three types of scoters found in the North Pacific, this diving duck lives most of its life in the sea along the coast. Only the males have the large yellow enlargement on their bills. Scoters feed by diving underwater. Black scoters feed mainly on blue mussels, clams, barnacles and other invertebrates. They nest in western and central Alaska near lakes and ponds.

Melanitta americana

Length: 17–21 inches
Weight: 29–45 ounces

Glaucous-winged Gull

Several kinds of gulls live along the North Pacific coast. Glaucous-winged Gulls are one of the largest and most common. They are identified by their size, white bodies with a light grey back and wings, pink legs, and yellow bill with a red spot. These gulls nest on offshore islands, but spend winter scouting for food all along the ocean shores. They eat mostly fish and marine invertebrates, as well as eggs and young of other birds, small mammals, dead animals and human garbage.

Larus glaucescens

Length: 24–27 inches
Weight: 31–42 ounces

33

Crucial Connections Around the World

Dr. Robert Paine coined the term, "keystone" as a name for top predators that shape the ecosystems in which they occur. Inspired by his research and the keystone species concept, ecologists began to look much more carefully at the connections that exist everywhere in nature. They soon realized that top predators are not the only individual species that can affect entire ecosystems.

Investigations from every continent, from the high arctic to the antarctic, revealed that one single species is often surprisingly important. A plant, a mammal, a bird, a fish, a tiny insect or marine invertebrate, even a fungus or bacteria, may be critically significant. The size or kind of organism isn't relevant. What matters are all the invisible connections between that species and the other creatures in the ecosystem in which it lives. Any single species with many tight, or unique, connections to another species, or a host of other creatures, could be a species whose abundance, or extinction, may determine the fate of many other species, or even an entire ecosystem.

In general use, all such species are often called "keystones," but ecologists now also use other terms to convey information about why any particular species is uniquely important. Understanding the many ties among diverse organisms and the environments where they live requires years of study. And most connections in nature remain unstudied. However, scientists have identified a variety of individual species that affect entire ecosystems, including the following examples.

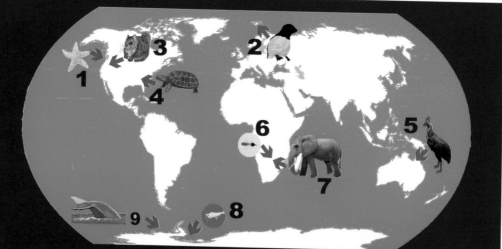

1. Ochre Sea Star
   Pisaster ochreace
2. Dovekie *Alle alle*
3. Northern Flying Squirrel
   Glaucomys sabrinus
4. Gopher Tortoise *Gopherus polyphemus*
5. Southern Cassowary *Casuarius casuarius*
6. Mound-building Termite
   Macrotermes michaelseni
7. African Elephant *Loxodonta africana*
8. Antarctic Krill *Euphausia superba*
9. Blue Whale *Balaenoptera musculus*

Dovekie (Little Auk) *Alle alle*

Long, cold, dark winters in the high arctic limit plant growth. Yet on the island of Svalbard, Norway, certain hillsides are carpeted by lichens, grasses, and flowers during summer. These unusually rich areas provide habitat for reindeer, barnacle geese, arctic foxes, and various small birds and insects. These rich areas exist only because they lie beneath the nesting colonies of a small seabird, the dovekie or little auk. Tens of thousands of these birds feed out at sea, but nest in the rock crevices of Svalbard's mountain slopes. While flying to and from their nests, the dovekies offload nitrogen-rich droppings which fertilize the tundra. This allows plants to grow and flourish where they otherwise could not exist. Due to the connections between the dovekies and the tundra plants, several other species can flourish on this arctic island.

Northern Flying Squirrel
Glaucomys sabrinus

Biologists identified the northern flying squirrel as a critical species in evergreen forests of northwestern North America. You aren't likely to see one if you visit these forests because this squirrel is only active at night. They glide down from the trees to dig up and feed on underground fungi. These fungi form a vast underground network which the trees in the forest depend on to help them absorb minerals from the soil. Since these fungi rely on flying squirrels to spread throughout the forest, the health and longtime survival of the trees, and the entire forest ecosystem, depends on the continued activities of these small, nocturnal mammals.

35

Gopher Tortoise *Gopherus polyphemus*

In the longleaf pine forests of the southeastern United States, over 300 animal species use underground burrows for shelter from fires, extreme weather, and to avoid predators. The gopher tortoise is one of very few species that digs out these underground shelters. Indigo snakes, rattlesnakes, gopher frogs, and burrowing owls are among the many animals that depend on the gopher tortoise burrows. With powerful clawed forelimbs, this tortoise digs long deep tunnels in the sandy ground. Some burrows measure up to 45 feet in length! The tortoises spend much of their lives in these burrows, emerging mainly to feed and find mates.

Southern Cassowary
Casuarius casuarius

The cassowary, the second largest bird in the world, is a critical species in the rainforest of northeast Australia. This giant, flightless bird is the only animal that can eat the big fruits of several unique tree species. By eating these fruits and then spreading the seeds in their droppings, cassowaries help the trees reproduce and spread. Without the cassowary, several tree species would eventually die out and disappear from the forest. And without the trees, the many Australian animals that depend upon them for food and shelter would soon disappear too.

Mound-building Termite *Macrotermes michaelseni*

In the savannas of east Africa, ecologists have identified two very different crucially important species - termites and African elephants. The 10 to 30 feet tall structures created by colonies of the mound-building termite provide food and shelter for a variety of animals, including barbets and mongooses. More importantly, these termites build extensive underground tunnels and farm fungi that break down wood and other plant material the termites gather. These actions enrich the soil with nutrients and allow water and air to seep into the ground more readily. This creates the right soil conditions for several kinds of trees and shrubs that could not otherwise grow in the dry, nutrient-poor soil. A variety of insects, birds and small mammals find food and shelter in these trees and shrubs. Several large browsing mammals, like elephants, giraffes, and certain antelope, need the trees and shrubs as a food source.

African Elephant *Loxodonta africana*

Many animals that live in the savanna, such as zebras, cape buffalo, wildebeests, and gazelles, don't need trees, they require grasses and herbs. That is partly why the African elephant is also considered critically important in this ecosystem. These giant animals eat and knock down tress and shrubs, preventing these plants from eventually crowding out most grasses. Elephants also spread the seeds of a variety of plants in their droppings. They use  their tusks to dig deep into the ground, thus creating waterholes that benefit many other animals. The astounding variety of plant-eating animals that thrive in the savanna provide food for leopards, lions, wild dogs, and other predators. All of these animals are food for scavengers–hyenas, vultures, and dung beetles among others. Without both termites and elephants, the amazingly rich savanna ecosystems of east Africa would not be home to anywhere near the great diversity of species that currently inhabit this remarkable environment.

Antarctic Krill

Euphausia superba

A small marine invertebrate, the Antarctic krill, is the primary food for most of the penguin, seal, and whale species that live in the icy cold environment of Antarctica. Antarctic animals that don't eat the krill, eat other animals that do. Without the krill, nearly all wildlife of Antarctica would suffer famine and likely soon disappear. Antarctic krill are clearly another example of one single species that affects an entire ecosystem.

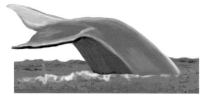

Blue Whale *Balaenoptera musculus*

The comparatively rare blue whale is also a singularly important species in the Southern Ocean. Plankton are the primary food of krill. They can flourish only in iron-rich waters, but this mineral is scarce in surface waters of Antarctica. By feeding at depth, then returning to the surface to breathe and release their iron-rich body wastes, blue whales stimulate rich blooms of plankton. More plankton results in higher populations of krill, which in turn, provides more food for all the animals that eat krill. Some evidence indicates that when blue whales were over-hunted and became rare in the Southern Ocean, krill also became less abundant. So, ironically, krill populations may indirectly depend on one of the animals that eat them.

Scientists have barely begun to unravel all the complex connections among the millions of species in nature. The more they learn, the more clearly they understand how much we humans do not yet know about how nature works and the values of any one single species.

About the author & illustrator

"I am intrigued by nature and science and aim to help others of all ages discover and appreciate the beauty and complexity of our world."

Susan E. Quinlan

An award-winning writer of science books for young readers, Susan E. Quinlan has studied and explored nature in diverse environments around the world, from the high arctic to Antarctica, from deserts to tropical rainforests.

Trained as a wildlife biologist, she conducted field research on seabirds, songbirds and bird migration in Alaska, then worked several years as a naturalist guide for Lindblad Expeditions.

Susan creates art to share her love of nature using watercolor, fused glass, fabric, batik and digital media.

For teacher's guides, posters, and more information, visit www.susanquinlan.com

Additional Books by Susan E. Quinlan

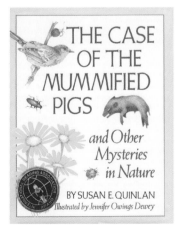

Revised edition coming soon

A collection of fourteen ecological mystery stories. Each stand-alone chapter details the investigative steps taken by scientists leading to the discovery of a surprising natural connection. In the next best thing to hands-on experience, readers learn about the scientific process and some of the remarkable hidden connections in nature.

A Junior Literary Guild Selection
International Reading Association Children's Book Award
National Science Teachers Association Outstanding Science Book
Skipping Stones Book Award for Nature and Ecology Books
Kansas State Reading Circle Selection

Follow the steps of investigating scientists as they try to figure out what is going on in the tropical forests of Central and South America. Why would several howler monkeys suddenly fall from the trees? How do tiny frogs make deadly poisons? Why do certain plants always harbor swarms of biting ants? Why would butterflies follow around predatory army ants? Readers discover how scientists search for clues and ultimately learn about a few of the amazing connections in tropical ecosystems.

A Junior Literary Guide Selection
Natural History Magazine Selection for Young Readers
National Science Teachers Association Outstanding Science Book Selection

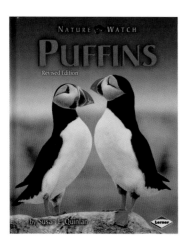

Best known for their clown-like appearance, puffins are remarkable seabirds with adaptations that enable them to live out at sea, far from land. Discover how these unusual birds are able to keep warm, survive drinking saltwater and catch fish and other prey. Learn about their amazing nesting colonies, strange courtship behaviors, and unusual nesting habits. Find out why the future of these amazing birds is uncertain and how to help ensure their future.

Parents' Choice Nonfiction Recommendation
Children's Choice Award
Teachers' Choice Award

Caribou are a type of deer that roam the forests and tundra of Earth's northernmost lands. Learn about their life history and discover the unique adaptations that enable caribou to survive in harsh northern environments. How do they keep warm in extreme cold, find food buried in deep snow, travel thousands of miles across rugged terrain and wild rivers? How do they survive in spite of hordes of mosquitoes and predation by wolves, bears, and wolverines?

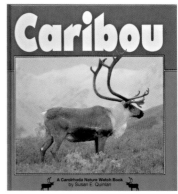

National Science Teachers Association Outstanding Science Book Selection

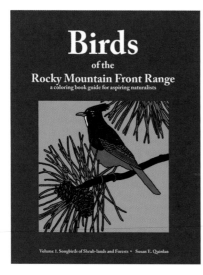

Learn about common birds of the Rocky Mountain Front Range. Line drawing illustrations to color, full-color coloring guide, and identification and natural history information about each bird. Tips for beginning bird watchers.

Vol. 1. Birds of Shrublands and Forests
From hummingbirds and woodpeckers to warblers, sparrows and grosbeaks, color and learn to identify the traits of 48 common birds of front range shrublands and forests.

Vol. 2. Birds of Rivers, Lakes and Marshlands
Coming soon...From grebes to shorebirds, gulls through waterfowl, color and learn to identify the traits of common birds of front range wetland habitats.